Property Rights and the Environment

Giuliano d'Auria
Nicola Tynan
Catherine Gillespie
Joseph Thomas

Published by the IEA Environment Unit, 1999

First published in March 1999 by
The Environment Unit
The Institute of Economic Affairs
2 Lord North Street
Westminster
London SW1P 3LB

IEA Studies on the Environment No. 13
All rights reserved
ISBN 0 255 36471-7

Many IEA publications are translated into languages other than English or are reprinted. Permission to translate or to reprint should be sought from the General Director at the address above.

Printed in Great Britain by
Hartington Fine Arts Limited, Lancing, West Sussex
Set in Times New Roman and Univers

Contents

	Foreword	*Julian Morris*	5
	Introduction	*John Blundell*	7
	The Authors		10
1.	The Importance of Poperty Rights, the Market Order and the Rule of Law in Protecting the Environment		13
		Giuliano d'Auria	
2.	How to Have Your Seahorse and Eat It: Conservation of a Common Pool Resource		24
		Nicola Tynan	
3.	Protecting the Environment with Property Rights, the Market and the Rule of Law: The Case of Norilsk		36
		Catherine Gillespie	
4.	No More Toxic Beach Parties: The State of Britain's Beaches		46
		Joseph Thomas	
	Summary		*Back Cover*

Foreword

The idea that private enforcement of property rights might be a useful tool in protecting the environment is not new: Ronald Coase, Harold Demsetz and Armen Alchian each made significant contributions to our understanding of this issue in the 1960s; Terry Anderson, P.J. Hill, Elinor Ostrom and others continued this work in the 1970s and after. However, university courses and textbooks in environmental and resource economics rarely pay more than lip-service to this important idea. Indeed, the standard analysis typically assumes away any role for private enforcement of property rights. Coase's analysis is spuriously characterised as requiring zero transaction costs (the 'Coase Theorem') or being irrelevant beyond cases involving very small numbers. These analyses typically assume that transaction costs will be too large for individuals to discover solutions through law and markets, yet I have never seen any attempt to justify this assumption empirically. Just how large are the transaction costs involved and how large do they have to be to obviate private solutions? Of course, we all know that monitoring and enforcing property rights are costly activities, but one of the great insights of the work of Anderson and Hill in particular is that if people have *de jure* rights, then they will find innovative solutions that enable them also to have *de facto* rights. To ignore this fact implies a prejudice against the market that is not only unjustifiable but also frankly harmful to future developments in environmental protection. Teaching students that regulatory intervention (albeit using 'market-based instruments') is almost always necessary in order to solve environmental problems will perpetuate this prejudice and result in less efficient and less equitable solutions to these problems.

In light of the dominance of the anti-market view, it was a great pleasure, as one of the judges of this year's Annual John B. Wood Memorial Essay Competition, to see so many fine essays demonstrating a deep understanding of the role of property rights in providing solutions to environmental problems. Although the very high calibre of the essays made selection of winners difficult, it made the decision to publish them a no-brainer.

The essays contained herein are the four that were judged to be of the highest calibre out of all the entrants. The essays by Giuliano d'Auria and Joseph Thomas provide theoretical explanations as to why property rights and the rule of law protect the environment. The essay by Catherine Gillespie provides a practical example of what happens both when private property rights are not defined and enforced and what happens when they are. The essay by Nicola Tynan shows why trade restrictions are not an effective means for conserving species, whereas private property rights are.

As with all Institute publications, the opinions are those of the authors alone and not of the Institute (which has no corporate view), its Trustees, Advisers or Directors.

March 1999 JULIAN MORRIS
Director, IEA Environment Unit

Introduction

John B. Wood was a remarkable man.

In mid-1986 I interviewed Nobel Laureate Dr Milton Friedman for an article[1] I was writing to mark the 30th anniversary of the founding of the Institute of Economic Affairs (IEA). I asked him what accounted for the IEA's huge impact on British opinion. High on his list of factors was the often unsung contribution of John Wood.

After studying Philosophy, Politics and Economics at Oxford and Economics at Cambridge, John's career started in the civil service. He went on to politics, journalism, the city and industry before a move to the IEA's staff part-time in 1969 and then full-time as Deputy Director in 1971, a position he filled for two decades.

But while most remember John as the quiet administrator, he also played key roles as an IEA Trustee in the sixties and as author or co-author of important IEA titles in the seventies and early eighties. These include:

- *How Much Unemployment?*, Research Monograph No. 28, April 1972;

- *How Much Inequality?*, with George Polanyi, Research Monograph No. 31, June 1974;

- *How Little Unemployment?*, Hobart Paper No. 65, October 1975;

- *Exchange Control for Ever?*, with Robert Miller, Research Monograph No. 33, February 1979;

---

[1] 'How to Move a Nation', *Reason*, February 1987.

- 'How it all Began – Personal Recollections', in *The Emerging Consensus?*, edited by Arthur Seldon, June 1981; and

- *What Price Unemployment? An Alternative Approach*, with Robert Miller, Hobart Paper No. 92, January 1982 (Second Impression: September 1983; Third Impression: March 1984; and Fourth Impression: February 1985).

Above all, his *Exchange Control for Ever?*, published in February 1979, clearly heralded Sir Geoffrey Howe's daring October 1979 repeal. Indeed one of John's finest moments must have been when, with co-author Robert Miller, he was toasted by Howe and co-minister Nigel Lawson at a post-repeal party hosted by Sir Michael Richardson, then head of Corporate Finance at Rothschilds.

John died very unexpectedly in late summer 1991 while undergoing routine surgery. In his memory his brother Hugh has generously funded an annual essay contest for young people on topics close to John's heart.

Over the years entrants from around the world have penned 3,000 word essays galore on topics from arts policy to macro-economics to the environment. Each year the prize money has been generous (up to US$5,000) and each year the IEA has retained the right to publish the winning entries.

However, what sets the Class of '98 apart is that it is the biggest field to date, the best field to date and the closest field to date. It is also the first time that the IEA has exercised its option to publish the winning entries. Indeed the field was so close that we are publishing four rather than three winners because we had two tie for first and two tie for third.

Entrants in this sixth annual contest were asked to write on one of the following:

- An environmental problem, showing how a property rights approach can provide solutions; or

- The importance of property rights, the market order and the rule of law in protecting the environment; or

- A book review of *Down to Earth II: Combating Environmental Myths* by Matt Ridley.

Why the environment, who are the winners and what did they write?

The environment has become the key battlefield in the war of ideas between the top down, command and control, dirigiste regulators on the one hand and the bottom up, rule of law, decentralised free-marketeers on the other. It is a critically important debate, a debate which will determine how our children and grand children live their lives.

The winners of the 1998 contest were:

Joint First Place

Mr Giuliano d'Auria, Research Physicist, Chloride Silectron, Bologna:
The Importance of Property Rights, the Market Order and the Rule of Law in Protecting the Environment.

Ms Nicola Tynan, PhD candidate, George Mason University, Fairfax, VA:
How to Have Your Seahorse and Eat It: Conservation of a Common Pool Resource.

Joint Third Place

Ms Catherine Gillespie, Financial Analyst, Société Générale, London:
Protecting the Environment with Property Rights, the Market and the Rule of Law: The Case of Norilsk.

Mr Joseph Thomas, Energy Analyst, Datamonitor, London:
No More Toxic Beach Parties: The State of Britain's Beaches.

March 1999 JOHN BLUNDELL
General Director, Institute of Economic Affairs

The Authors

Giuliano d'Auria was born in Rome and graduated in physics at Rome University in 1995. He spent two years working in scientific research, winning several scholarships in the field of optics and contributing to articles published in specialised journals. He is currently working in industry for the electronics multinational Chloride Silectron in Bologna, Italy. His major interests lie in the field of economics with a strong focus on the Austrian School.

Nicola Tynan graduated with a BSc in economics from York University in 1991, after which she worked briefly as a research journalist on *The Banker* magazine. From 1993 to 1996 Ms Tynan was development officer for the Institute of Economic Affairs. During this time, she also taught undergraduate economics at City University Business School and obtained a Master's degree in political theory from the LSE.

Ms Tynan is currently a graduate student in the Department of Economics at George Mason University, where she is completing a doctoral dissertation on 'Competition and the Private Provision of Water'. She also acts as a consultant to the World Bank on private water projects in developing countries.

Catherine Gillespie was born in Devon and graduated with a BSc in economics from the LSE in 1997. Her essay was written whilst she was working at the *Institutional Investor*, writing for 'Emerging Markets Week'. Since September of last year, she has been an analyst at Société Générale, covering emerging markets country funds.

Joseph Thomas graduated from the LSE in 1997. He worked at the Center for Market Processes in Fairfax, VA as a Koch Fellow in summer 1997, where he was first prize winner in the group research project on social security reform. He carried out research for the recently published book, *Public Spending* by Evan Davis, the Economics Editor of Newsnight, and is currently employed as an Energy Analyst for Datamonitor, a market analysis company in London.

1. The Importance of Property Rights, the Market Order and the Rule of Law in Protecting the Environment

Giuliano d'Auria

Having seen their ideas miserably fail in the field of economic management, advocates of command and control methods have turned to the environment in a desperate attempt to seek support and credibility for their theories. All environmental problems are treated by the environment protection business as evidence of market failure and therefore justifying direct State intervention and control of the environment.

Externalities, which include the effects an activity or an exchange has on people other than the parties directly involved, figure prominently in all arguments over market failure. From the criticisms made by environmentalists it is possible to identify two forms of externalities depending on whether the external spillovers affect current property rights holders or future generations.

Unpriced spillover effects between the activities of different individuals cause private costs to diverge from social costs and the scale of the activities to differ from the optimal level consistent with the maximisation of social welfare. These externalities are blamed for causing everything from pollution of the atmosphere and deforestation to the depletion of natural resources and the degradation of open spaces. All these diverse environmental threats are alleged to spring from a common origin: the inability of producers in a capitalist system to bear the entire costs of their activities.

A close examination of the list of environmental problems facing the world reveals, however, that capitalism is prominent for its absence since environmental threats are found in areas, such as the sea and the atmosphere, where private property rights are not present. Far from providing evidence of market failure, externalities demonstrate the failures of State intervention since they occur where free market principles are not applied. A close look at these principles should make it apparent that negative externalities and capitalism are contradictions in terms since spillovers represent a form of aggression on private property which is contrary to the spirit of liberalism. Pollution, which is a classic example of externality caused by production, represents a blatant invasion of private property rights and is therefore incompatible with the free market (Piombini, 1996).

The problems posed by externalities and conflicts between property rights have traditionally been dealt with in liberal societies through the common law and the law of nuisance in particular. Courts may stop nuisance by ordering a defendant to pay damages or by issuing an injunction that stops the defendant from generating the nuisance. In either case the law of nuisance defines property rights and sets the stage for bargaining to take place between the parties to discover the optimal level of nuisance and internalise the externality. This is the point made by Coase in his famous theorem which states that, provided transaction costs are negligible, the efficiency of the bargaining process is not affected by the initial assignment of entitlement (Coase, 1960).

The efficiency of contractual agreements between consenting individuals has, however, been undermined by the collectivist philosophy with its belief in the common good of society achieved through the nationalisation of the bargaining process. This philosophy has led the State to abandon its traditional role of enforcing property rights and the law, while claiming a monopoly in balancing the nuisance caused by economic activities with the benefits derived from production. Free agreements reached by contract and consent have been replaced by the imposition of outcomes by command and control. In its vain attempt to control the environment the State has therefore adopted methods which have demonstrably failed in the field of economics, as the collapse of socialist countries has shown.

The basic fallacy of command and control methods springs from the superficial belief that the order we observe in society derives from the imposition of exogenous forces. Once we accept

Hayek's teaching that society is a spontaneous order formed from endogenous forces, it should become apparent that we have less power and control over it than human arrogance may wish to pretend. This is because a spontaneous order contains more dispersed knowledge and information than any single person could possibly master or control (Hayek, 1960).

Since the general principles embodied in common law operate by altering incentives while allowing individuals full use of their personal knowledge, they are far more effective in influencing behaviour towards the environment than command and control methods, which naively assume a one to one connection between command (legislation) and outcome. This is evident in the law of tort, which allows victims to seek compensation for damages and therefore represents a constant deterrence to negligent behaviour. The effectiveness of common law in controlling pollution and encouraging adequate precaution has, however, been undermined by the expansion of national statutes. In Britain the rights to fish a particular part of a lake or stream are privately held and owners may take legal action against polluters who harm their fishing grounds. This system of liability in common law is far more effective in protecting the environment than any national statute could ever be and helped to keep rivers clean long before the growth of green movements.

The preservation of the environment into the future can be undermined by temporal externalities which unload spillovers on to future generations. The desire to protect the environment for the sake of these generations can only be sustained if time preferences are high and the existing institutional arrangements induce individuals to place a high value on the future.

Alchian has observed that the kind of behaviour and attitudes people follow depend on the allocation system in force, which is in turn connected to the existing system of property rights (Alchian, 1967). Common property implies an allocation system based on the 'first come first served' principle. We therefore observe that the absence of property rights triggers off a scramble to be first comer since second comers have no certainty of finding anything left. The lack of certainty over the future leads first comers to consume the entire resource as if there were no tomorrow. This overexploitation inherent in a system of common ownership has been described by Hardin as the 'tragedy of the commons, and is responsible for the depletion of the fish stock, the extinction of wildlife and deforestation to name but a few examples. (Hardin, 1968). The poaching of rhinos almost to extinction exemplifies the close to infinite disregard for the future displayed by poachers in their rush to be first comers and contrasts sharply with the long term interest and care taken by farmers for their animals ('t Sas-Rolfes, 1995).

The investment required for the protection of the environment will only be forthcoming if the future is highly valued. Property rights inspire the confidence in the future which induces owners to internalise it into their present behaviour.

Confidence in the future is also favoured by the establishment of the rule of law which, by limiting the use of arbitrary coercion, allows time horizons to be relaxed inducing greater concern for the effects present actions have on the future. Law and order, by minimising the likelihood of future conflicts, also plays an important role in building up confidence and tilting time profiles away from the short run. The general uncertainty generated by State meddling has the opposite effect and contributes to the high discounting of the future and bias towards the short run which is so destructive of the environment.

Free market critics often make the point that property owners are moved, not by their concern for the long term state of their property, but by the possibility of making a quick profit by selling their rights when their value is high. This argument fails to appreciate that it is the transferability of property rights that causes the capitalisation of future effects on to present values. The prospect of capturing value gains from the improved marketable value of resources induces owners to take care of their property, and channel investment into its protection. Moreover, the transferability of property rights translates market incentives into an automatic conservation mechanism, since the threat of future shortages encourages resource owners to preserve their property so as to gain from the prospect of its increased future value.

Although property rights are inherently efficient and environmentally friendly since they allow the internalisation of both the future and external spillovers, their establishment requires enforcement costs which hinder their development. Private ownership will only be observed if the benefits derived from property rights exceed the costs incurred enforcing them. The evolution of property rights therefore closely matches the ever changing balance of benefits and costs.

The benefits which can be derived from ownership depend in the first place on the value of the economic goods: the higher the value the greater the potential benefit. Since value is affected by availability, the investment worth making to enforce property claims will increase with scarcity. This means that the market channels investments towards the natural resources which most need protection.

Scarcity is not the only element affecting value. Since the marketability of resources affects their future earning prospects, it also has a direct effect on the investment worth making to protect the natural goods. All measures aimed at discouraging trade in environmental goods (trade bans, regulations, fines, etc.) decrease the value of the resources and hence the investment going into their protection. For this reason the ban on trading in rhino products and ivory, far from protecting rhinos and elephants, diverts resources away from their conservation. A sensible policy to protect endangered species would therefore attempt to maximise the profits made from trading in the species by opening up new markets and developing institutions facilitating their commercialisation.

Demsetz provides us with an extremely interesting analysis in which he attributes the establishment of land rights for the hunting of fur animals (beavers in particular) among American Indians of the Labrador Peninsula to the development of the fur trade (Demsetz, 1967). The opening up of this new market led to a sharp increase in the value of fur which by the beginning of the eighteenth century tilted the balance of costs and benefits towards the establishment of property rights.

The costs incurred in enforcing property rights depend on the nature of the economic goods, the state of technology and the presence of an established legal framework. The implication of this argument is that the absence of property rights in the past is not a reason for excluding their development in the future since both technology and legal institutions may change.

This observation is specially relevant for all those collective goods which are assumed to possess the quality of non-excludability (meaning that it is unpractical to prevent non-payers from consuming these goods). Environmental amenities are generally included among these goods which the market is supposedly unable to provide because of the free-rider problem: individuals are under no pressure to contribute to their provision since non-payers cannot be excluded.

Free-riding is traditionally taken as a justification for the direct State provision and protection of environmental goods. However, what may have appeared as non-excludable in the past may later become an excludable good as a result of the lowering of the cost of enforcing the rights brought about by technological advance. Private ownership may thus move into the realm of possibilities. The development of land rights in the American far west provides us with a classic example of this process (Anderson and Hill, 1975). When the commons in England were enclosed, the planting of hedges appeared the most obvious way of defining the land rights. This solution proved totally inadequate for the huge expanses of land in the American far west which therefore remained open range. It was only with the invention of barbed wire in the 1870s that the opportunity of defining land rights in the far west was offered and private grazing could be introduced.

There is no limit to human inventiveness and ingenuity in the struggle to overcome the tragedy of the commons, and the opportunities opened by technology are truly impressive.

Open access to valuable sea resources is commonly regarded as an inevitable consequence of the nature of the sea which supposedly epitomises non-excludability. Although this may have been a valid description when the cost of monitoring and enforcing rights on sea resources was prohibitively high, advances in technology are now tilting incentives towards the establishment of property rights. This tendency is clearly visible in the privately owned oyster beds in the USA or the artificial reefs built by Japanese fisherman to encourage the growth of fishery resources. The phenomenal growth of aquaculture is also evidence of the failure of the common access system to ensure long term sustainability (De Alessi, 1996).

Although it is certainly true that private ownership is only observed when the balance of benefits and costs is positive, this does not in itself provide an explanation for its development. The evolution of property rights is not automatic and only results from a discovery process in which entrepreneurial individuals grasp the opportunities offered by the ownership of scarce resources. The changing balance of costs and benefits merely provides the information and incentives for the creative discoveries of ever changing opportunities offered by changing scarcities, technologies and preferences. This interpretation, which forms the centrepiece of the Austrian School of Economics, was first exposed by Hayek (Hayek, 1949) and further developed by Kirzner (Kirzner, 1992) in his criticism of the 'given pie' perspective according to which all resources, including information and knowledge, are assumed to be given and readily available. Although resources given by nature can obviously be said to exist physically, their economic value is only established through a process of entrepreneurial discovery triggered by the opportunities offered by the prospect of gain. So it was that oil turned from being a slimy black fluid at the beginning of the nineteenth century to become the black gold of the twentieth century. The implication of this argument is that from an economic point of view resources are never 'given pies', but the creation of entrepreneurial discoveries.

This argument provides us with an explanation for the dismal failure of all the dire predictions made by environmental doomsayers going back to Malthus, warning us of the increasing scarcity of natural resources. The late Julian Simon has shown that the availability of natural resources has actually been increasing over the centuries since their price, which is the only meaningful indication of scarcity, has been on a secular downward trend (Simon, 1981). Relative to wages the cost of copper, which is representative of all metals, is only about a tenth of what it was two hundred years ago and about a thousand times lower than it was in Babylonia some 4000 years ago. This apparent paradox is solved once we abandon the given pie assumption and accept that resources are not fixed but come into existence through creative discoveries. Although in the short run resources are limited, price rises induced by impending shortages present an opportunity for profit minded entrepreneurs to discover new resources or to invent substitutes.

The discovery process explains why in the course of history property rights have expanded to include patents, copyrights and trade marks and how they could further develop as individuals discover the increased value of threatened natural resources and the benefits which can be derived from their protection. The opportunities offered by the private protection of the environment will, however, only be discovered if the incentives and information communicated by the market order and the price system are not distorted by State intervention.

The extension of private ownership to hitherto untouched areas may be facilitated by the discovery of new forms of ownership and contractual agreements which open the way to previously precluded exchanges. By reshuffling and developing the bundle of rights defining property new combinations and new institutional arrangements may be formed, providing innovative solutions to the problems posed by externalities.

Easements and covenants are two examples of how property rights may be redefined by imposing conditions and requirements on owners so as to control external effects in the use of land. Whereas easements give rights to one landowner to make some use of another's property, covenants impose requirements on a landowner to take some kind of action. In either case the bundle of rights defining property is reshuffled and a new right is devised allowing the control of the general environment without resorting to zoning laws and central planning of the use of land. The development of Houston, Texas, which has until recently entirely relied on these market transactions, demonstrates the feasibility and effectiveness of market alternatives to the direct control of the environment by the State.

In a world free from distorting interferences, property rights and legal institutions develop to meet the challenges presented by environmental problems. Undistorted markets have, however, been in short supply throughout history and it is therefore difficult to imagine what institutions might have developed if only governments had not distorted the incentives and information on which discoveries are based. Hayek suggests that the conflicts of interest arising out of land use would probably have led to a division between holders of superior and inferior rights (Hayek, 1960). Whereas owners of superior rights would determine the overall character of large districts, the detailed development of smaller units of land would be left to the inferior rights holders. This distribution of rights would probably have opened the way to the development of private cities and avoided the need for State management of the environment.

The devolution of rights to local communities can give rise to institutional arrangements combining aspects of both public and private goods. This compromise may solve the problems posed by pure public goods when the social groups are small and cohesive, as in the case of condominiums or meadow land in Switzerland. Community-based management of wildlife has also proved an effective mid-way solution, as the CAMPFIRE projects in Zimbabwe have shown (Sugg and Kreuter, 1994).

The bundle of rights defining property can vary from a system of almost complete open access to total private control. The discovery of the optimal combination forms an integral part of the market process and, if left unhindered, leads inexorably towards the extension of property rights and away from the tragedy of the commons.

References

Armen A. Alchian (1967): *Pricing and Society*, London: Institute of Economic Affairs, Occasional Paper 17.

Terry L. Anderson and P. J. Hill (1975): 'The Evolution of Property Rights: A Study of the American West', *Journal of Law and Economics*, 18, pp. 163-179.

Ronald H. Coase (1960): 'The Problem of Social Cost', *Journal of Law and Economics*, 3(1).

Michael De Alessi (1996): *Emerging Technologies and Private Stewardship of Marine Resources*, London: Institute of Economic Affairs, Environment Unit Working Paper No. 1.

H. Demsetz (1967): 'Towards a Theory of Property Rights', *American Economic Review*, 57, pp. 347-59.

Garrett Hardin (1968): 'The Tragedy of the Commons', *Science*, pp. 1244-45.

Friedrich A. Hayek (1949): 'The Use of Knowledge in Society', in *Individualism and Economic Order*, London: Routledge & Kegan Paul.

Friedrich A. Hayek (1960): *The Constitution of Liberty*, London: Routledge.

Israel M. Kirzner (1992): 'Discovery, Private Property and the Theory of Justice in Capitalist Society', in *The Meaning of Market Process*, London: Routledge.

Guglielmo Piombini (1996): 'Per un Ecologismo Liberista', in *Federalismo & Società*, III, 3.

Julian L. Simon (1981): *The Ultimate Resource*, Princeton, NJ : Princeton University Press.

Ike Sugg and Urs Kreuter (1994): *Elephants and Ivory: Lessons from the Trade Ban*, London: Institute of Economic Affairs, Studies on the Environment No. 2.

Michael 't Sas-Rolfes (1995): *Rhinos: Conservation, Economics and Trade-Offs*, London: Institute of Economic Affairs, Studies on the Environment No. 4.

2. How to Have Your Seahorse and Eat It: Conservation of a Common Pool Resource

Nicola Tynan

Abstract

Seahorses are under threat. They are over-fished and populations are diminishing. This paper argues that seahorse over-fishing presents a problem for producers, consumers, and environmentalists. Wildlife conservation groups call for trade bans or quotas. Neither of these will solve the problem.

Fishermen in one Philippine village have found a way to protect the seahorse. They use communal property rights and private enforcement to protect the local seahorse population and simultaneously secure their own future as fishermen. This paper shows how this and other property rights solutions will keep the seahorse from extinction.

Introduction

Natural history TV documentaries allow viewers to watch animals in their natural environment while simultaneously learning about the animal from an expert. The scientists who present these documentaries know their own subject intimately, but few presenters' expertise extends to political, social and economic issues. When addressing questions of environmental economics they do not research their topic thoroughly, but rely on their intuition.

The *Kingdom of the Seahorse* is an exception.[1] This documentary provides an example of a scientist both researching

---

[1] *Kingdom of the Seahorse* is a PBS/NOVA documentary written by and featuring Amanda Vincent. For the text of the program see NOVA's web site at http://www.pbs.org/wgbh/nova/seahorse.

her own subject thoroughly and investigating the impact of her policy suggestions. The presenter provides viewers with a sensible long-term solution to an environmental problem: the diminishing seahorse population in the Philippines.

Each showing of *Kingdom of the Seahorse* generates viewer interest in the seahorse. An interest in seahorses increases consumer demand for seahorses and increases seahorse fishing. On the other hand, an awareness of the diminishing seahorse population encourages support for environmental groups claiming to protect the seahorse.

When policies advocated by environmentalists fail to achieve their purported goals, viewer support for these policies has adverse consequences: it threatens rather than preserves the species. It is therefore important to know which environmental policies work and which do not. The next section of this paper explains why the trade bans and quotas advocated by many environmental groups fail.

The presenter of *Kingdom of the Seahorse* shows that policies succeed when they devolve responsibility for conservation away from government and towards seahorse fishermen. The third part of this paper explores the advantages of private responsibility for seahorse conservation in greater detail. It focuses on the importance of institutional incentives and the role of private and common property rights in preventing over-exploitation.

The Demand for Seahorses

Seahorses are a species of small fish that can be found in almost any coastal area with sea grass beds, mangroves, or coral reefs. The seahorse got its name because its head resembles that of a horse, although seahorses have a long tubular snout rather than a nose and mouth. At the other end of their body, seahorses have a long, spiral-ended tail that they wrap around soft coral or grass to anchor themselves as they search for prey. They use each of their eyes independently to scan the water for shrimp and tiny fish.

There are at least thirty-five species of seahorse world-wide, with one or two species living in each coastal location. Seahorse bodies are textured, often with spikes, to match their environment. As each seabed varies, so each species differs. Species come in a variety of colours, again determined by their environment, and many species change colour as their environment changes. Adult seahorses range from less than an inch to fourteen inches long, again depending on their species (Vincent, 1994).

It is common among fish for the male to raise and nurture the young, but the seahorse takes this role further. The seahorse provides one of only two known examples of male rather than female pregnancy. Female seahorses deposit their eggs in their partner's pouch for fertilisation. The male then carries his offspring for twenty-one days before releasing fully formed young into the sea.

Despite its uniqueness, the seahorse remains one of the least researched of all fish.[2] Only recently have scientists discovered that seahorses are unusual in another respect: they appear to form lifelong partnerships and they remain monogamous during each breeding season. The discovery of seahorse monogamy coincides with scientists' discovery that many other seemingly monogamous animals, particularly birds, do not remain faithful to their partners. (Because seahorses live far apart and are slow swimmers, monogamous bonding allows each seahorse to maximise its reproductive success – the major cause of unfaithfulness in other animals.)

Male pregnancy and a diversity of colour give seahorses a mystique that has created a consumer demand for seahorses and seahorse products. By far the strongest demand comes from Asian consumers, where seahorses form the basis of a large number of traditional Chinese medicines. China, Taiwan, Hong Kong, Singapore, Japan, Malaysia and South Korea are all major seahorse importers.[3] Traditional medicines are in particularly strong demand in Hong Kong, where men value their aphrodisiac quality. A chemist's shop in Hong Kong sells one dried kilogram of seahorse for about $1,200 (£700). As Chinese consumers in Hong Kong and mainland China have become wealthier in recent years, the demand for seahorses has grown rapidly. By the early

---

[2] Serious research started in 1986, when Dr Amanda Vincent began to study the seahorse for her PhD dissertation at the University of Oxford.

[3] See *TED Case Studies: Seahorse Trade* at http://gurukul.ucc.american.edu/ted/SEAHORSE.HTM

1990s the annual legal seahorse trade reached approximately 20 million, about 6 million (or 20 tons) of these going to consumers in China. The demand for seahorses in Asia has continued to increase.

Consumers in the USA, UK, Holland, and other Western countries share this fascination with seahorses and demand both dried and live seahorses. Dead seahorses are used for key rings and brooches, while live seahorses are bought for aquariums. The Philippines exported 200,000 seahorses to aquarium suppliers in the United States in 1987 and this demand for seahorses has grown in recent years. Seahorses are even available on the web from the 'virtual' pet shop Concept Aquatics at around $15 (£9) each – larger seahorses cost more, smaller ones cost less.[4]

The major seahorse exporting countries are the Philippines, Australia (south Australia and Tasmania), Thailand and China.[5] Although seahorse populations in these countries are not threatened by extinction now, there are signs that some populations are shrinking. The clearest sign is that the number of seahorses per catch is falling. In addition, the average size of seahorse per catch has fallen. The capture of smaller seahorses suggests a diminishing population because juvenile seahorses are being caught before being allowed to grow to full size and before breeding to restock the population.

In 1997 the environmental group TRAFFIC used this information on diminishing seahorse populations to persuade the European Community (EC) to place seahorses on Annex D of the new EC regulations on wildlife trade.[6] Annex D requires the

---

[4] See http://www.petstore.com/misc/yhorse.html

[5] Other seahorse exporting countries include Belize, Brazil, Indonesia, Kuwait, Malaysia, Mexico, Pakistan, Singapore, Tanzania, United Arab Emirates, United States and Vietnam.

[6] TRAFFIC International (Trade Records Analysis of Flora and Fauna in Commerce) is a joint program of WWF (World Wide Fund for Nature) and IUCN (World Conservation Union). In 1996, TRAFFIC published a 163-page report by Dr Vincent on the seahorse trade. Inclusion on the IUCN Red List signals that a species is vulnerable and makes future regulation more likely. Seahorse species were added to the list in 1996. At the United Nations' Rio Summit Convention for the research and conservation of threatened species in 1995, members agreed to provide a grant for research on the viability of the seahorse trade.

documentation of all imports or exports of seahorses in the EC. The next section of this paper argues against further EC or other government involvement in seahorse conservation.

Why Quotas Fail

Many environmental groups argue that trade quotas are the best way to protect species under threat, including the seahorse. Their argument assumes that reducing the number of seahorses legally traded will automatically reduce the number of seahorses fished. But a reduction in fishing is not guaranteed. The impact of trade restrictions on fishing behaviour depends on how the restrictions change the costs and benefits for each fisherman. This in turn depends on each fisherman's rights to current and future seahorse stocks.

Placing a ceiling on the number of seahorses traded will raise the price. This will make consumers in importing countries worse off; they will have to pay more for each seahorse they purchase. Seahorse exporters will receive more for each seahorse they sell, which appears to make them better off, but this need not be the case. The quota means that exporters will sell fewer seahorses. This fall in quantity sold could outweigh the rise in price and reduce the total income received by exporters. In this case the quota will make both buyers and sellers worse off, but it will reduce the number of seahorses sold.

The assumption that the supply of seahorses immediately falls to the level set by the quota erroneously treats seahorse exporters as a single entity when they are not. Each exporter acts independently and competes with other exporters to meet consumer demand. When faced with a quota, some exporters will fail to find a buyer but no exporter will voluntarily choose to reduce his sales.[7] The government agency imposing the quota must apportion it amongst the sellers. This process will waste resources as each exporter attempts to gain as much as possible

---

[7] This is slightly inaccurate. Each exporter could choose to reduce his time spent fishing by a small amount to enjoy a little more leisure and keep his income from seahorse sales the same. It is more likely, however, that he will sell at least as many horses to increase his income. In economic terminology, the substitution effect outweighs the income effect.

of the quota for himself, either through explicit bribes or implicit side-payments to government officials.

Buyers and sellers left out of the market after the imposition of a quota will attempt to get around the ban through black market trades. Seahorse fishermen will continue to supply seahorses until the costs of fishing plus the higher transactions costs of illegal trading equal the revenue they can get from selling seahorses on the black market. The higher transactions cost of illegal trading will not raise the quantity of seahorses traded to the pre-quota quantity, but will partially undermine the quota.

Quotas face another problem. A reduction in the number of seahorses traded will not necessarily reduce the number caught by fishermen. It could even increase the capture of seahorses. If governments limit the importation of seahorses, consumers will demand only the better seahorses. To ensure that his seahorses are the ones for which consumers are willing to pay the most, each fisherman will attempt to find as many as possible of the most valuable seahorses and will simply discard those of lower value, a practice known as highgrading (De Alessi, 1998, p. 47).[8] Regulatory uncertainty will encourage fishermen to behave in a way that acts against the intentions of the regulation. The imposition of a quota signals the possibility of further government intervention in the future. Any fisherman who receives a share of the quota or can sell seahorses on the black market now will make short-term profits, but each fisherman faces the prospect that reduced quotas or stricter enforcement in the future will raise the costs and drive him out of the market. This increases the value of an hour spent fishing now relative to an hour spent fishing in the future. Regulatory uncertainty encourages seahorse fishermen to catch more seahorses.

We already have an example of the failure of trade restrictions to reduce fishing. The importation into Taiwan of seahorses from China is illegal (under the general ban on imports from communist countries). An outright ban on trade is the same as a quota of zero, yet the trade still flourishes. The countries in

---

[8] The amount of highgrading is not easy to determine in advance. It will depend on the way in which the quota is apportioned amongst suppliers and the size of the black market.

which the trade bans are likely to succeed are those with stronger institutions for enforcement and regulation, those with less corruption. The bans are less likely to succeed in countries where seahorse populations are diminishing most rapidly because these countries have weak traditions of institutional monitoring and enforcement.

TRAFFIC has emphasised the role that trade plays in causing over-fishing. This emphasis is misplaced; the trade does not cause the over-fishing. Worse than being misplaced, TRAFFIC's emphasis on trade shifts attention away from the real problem: the over-fishing itself. Where quotas encourage heavier fishing in the short run, they undermine other efforts being made to address the problem of over-fishing.

Property Rights Solutions

Seahorse fishermen rely on the sale of seahorses for their income now and in the future. This gives them an interest in ensuring that the seahorse population does not diminish in a way that reduces their income in the future; the interests of fishermen, seahorses and environmentalists coincide. When each fisherman has no claim on future quantities of a natural resource, however, he has no motivation to conserve; any seahorses not caught by him now can be taken by others.

In economic terminology this problem is known as the 'tragedy of the commons', but it is not common ownership that causes the tragedy. Fishermen lose the motivation to conserve when property remains unowned (has open access) or is owned by the government (De Alessi, 1998, p. 13). Open access seahorse fishing allows anyone to fish in an area and effectively gives them ownership of each seahorse they catch. With open access no fisherman has an interest in the whole population of seahorses and its survival into the future; if this population disappears he will move on to another, and if he does not fish now other fishermen will.

At the other extreme, private ownership of a seahorse population will motivate the owner to ensure that current fishing does not reduce his income from seahorse fishing in the future. Private property rights usually refer to ownership of a good by one individual, but for common pool resources such as seahorse populations, ownership by a group can be more practical. The property rights approach to solving environmental problems focuses on institutional arrangements that encourage seahorse conservation and allow fishermen to continue selling seahorses.

The best form of property rights to protect seahorses will depend on each local situation. They range from a single outright owner of a seahorse farm to shared community ownership of a local seahorse population. In countries with weak traditions of property rights and where many families rely on the seahorses for their livelihood, collective institutions will dominate.

For resources with a small demand relative to their sustainable extraction, open access is not a problem. To reduce the number of seahorses caught would require someone to monitor fishermen and to enforce penalties on anyone over-fishing. These are both costly activities. When fishing remains within sustainable levels, incurring these costs is an unnecessary waste.

Small demand relative to sustainable extraction characterised the situation for seahorses for many years, and still does in some countries. When seahorse demand started to rise as a result of rising disposable income in China, Hong Kong and Taiwan, the situation changed. The costs of open access have increased to the point where the benefits of reducing fishing will outweigh the monitoring and enforcement costs.

In some countries villagers rely on the sale of seahorses as their main, or even sole, source of monetary income. This is true for a number of local communities in the Philippines. In 1990 a bulletin board in Germany claimed that the seahorse trade was the Philippines' most valuable fisheries export.[9] For some Philippine villagers the sale of seahorses provides their main source of monetary income.

One Philippine village whose members rely on the sale of seahorses is Handumon. Before 1995, fishermen in Handumon faced the classic commons problem: each fisherman aimed to catch as many seahorses as possible even when this threatened the future seahorse population. A few years ago each fisherman would return with a bucket full of seahorses on each trip. By

---

[9] See *TED Case Studies: Seahorse Trade.*

1995 he was lucky to return with more than a few in the bottom. Local fishermen estimate a reduction in the seahorse population between 50 per cent and 70 per cent from 1986 to 1996. The average size seahorse was also diminishing – a further sign of over-utilisation.

Before 1995 fishermen caught most of their fish in the sea just beyond their village, but fished freely in neighbouring areas when populations were higher there. Within the village each fisherman fished for himself and the support of his family; villagers did not act together to conserve the seahorse population. Some villagers did throw back pregnant males and individually monitored their behaviour, but the increased demand and falling supply put pressure on the less efficient fishermen not to do so. In 1995, the villagers admitted that unless they acted together their catch would continue to shrink.

With a small loan from an environmental organisation, villagers set up a sanctuary into which they agreed to put all pregnant males and juveniles. Now when a fisherman catches a juvenile seahorse, he sells it to the sanctuary for a small sum but retains his ownership claim to that seahorse. After the seahorse has grown to full size he buys it back for the same amount he sold it for, allowing him to sell the now larger seahorse for more on the market. Within a few months of setting up the sanctuary, the seahorse population in the area had started to grow, and with it the size of the catch. This brought the group's first problem: poachers.

Neighbouring communities had experienced the same reduction in seahorse populations. Handumon's greater supply now made poaching more profitable than local fishing. In retaliation, the people of Handumon set up a boat patrol to protect their property rights from outsiders. At first this outraged their neighbours; poaching had been an acceptable activity in the past. Once they realised that the Handumon people were serious, however, they turned to imitation. The Handumon fishermen moved beyond simply returning pregnant males to full-scale farming of the seahorses. Their successful example has attracted the interest of other village communities in the Philippines.

In her book, *Governing the Commons*, Elinor Ostrom gives examples of voluntary local solutions to collective action problems. Ostrom outlines eight key requirements for an institution to successfully solve the collective action problem in conserving a common pool resource (Ostrom, 1991, p. 4). These criteria include: clearly defined boundaries, congruence between appropriation rules and local conditions, and monitoring. Because the Handumon villagers have addressed these issues they have a good chance of succeeding. The greatest threat comes from the Philippine government. For the common-property arrangement in Handumon to survive the Philippine government must respect the villagers' rights to organise as they have, and allow them to protect their property from outsiders. So far they appear willing to do this.

Unfortunately, the idea of collective or private ownership of seahorses has not spread to other countries. In the US the seas around Florida remain government property, subject to conflicting regulations. While Florida fishermen compete with Philippine fishermen to meet the Chinese demand, the Philippine fishermen are pressured to maintain their level of supply.

Seahorses also die as non-seahorse fishermen in Florida catch them in their nets and throw them out (known in the literature as bycatch). Bycatch need not be a problem. It becomes one when fishermen are not able to sell their bycatch. When governments give fishermen non-tradable permits to sell only one species of fish, bycatch becomes worthless and they have no interest in ensuring the survival of bycatch species. In New Zealand the government has partially overcome the bycatch problem through the introduction of tradable permits, or Individual Transferable Quotas (ITQs). With ITQs the government determines the total catch of each species. This opens the way for short-term political motivations to dominate the long-run survival of each species when setting these totals.

Aquaculture offers another possibility for a private solution to diminishing seahorse populations. Scientists argue that seahorses are difficult to raise in captivity, but this has not prevented entrepreneurs from farming other animals. Scientists and environmentalists argued that turtles could not be raised in captivity, but for a number of years a group of entrepreneurs proved them wrong. Scientists have found seahorses difficult to raise in captivity because of their demand for live prey, predominantly shrimp. Since shrimp are already successfully farmed, environmentalists should not rule out the joint production of seahorses and shrimp.

Conclusion

Two major seahorse consumers, China and Hong Kong, have different institutional histories. Hong Kong's greater prosperity is a consequence of its adoption of British institutions of private property and free markets, while China suffered as a result of communal ownership and centralised control. Unfortunately, fisheries and oceans are one area where the British refuse to learn from their own institutional experience. European Union control of the waters around Britain through its Common Fisheries Policy provides an extreme example of government failure (De Alessi, 1998, pp. 35-9). By contrast, New Zealand's adoption of ITQs is a step towards private ownership. With this successful model close at hand for Asian seahorse exporters to follow, British environmentalists should not attempt to impose the mistaken European approach.

Fortunately, seahorses are still far from the threat of extinction. If British environmentalists start to learn from the failure of government regulation seahorses need never come close to that threat. Environmentalists should encourage the government to respect voluntary, property rights arrangements that make the interests of fishermen, consumers and environmentalists the same. This will ensure the survival of the seahorse.

References

Michael De Alessi (1998): *Fishing for Solutions*, London: Institute of Economic Affairs, Studies on the Environment No. 11.

Elinor Ostrom (1991): *Governing the Commons: The Evolution of Institutions for Collective Action*, Cambridge: Cambridge University Press, 1991.

Amanda C. J. Vincent (1994): 'The Improbable Seahorse', *National Geographic*, 186, 126-40, October.

Bibliography

Michael De Alessi (1996): *Emerging Technologies and the Private Stewardship of Marine Resources*, London: Institute of Economic Affairs, Environment Unit Working Paper No. 1.

'Don't Eat the Seahorses', *The Economist*, 98, 30 September 1995.

Matt Ridley (1996): *Down to Earth II: Combating Environmental Myths*, London: Institute of Economic Affairs, Studies on the Environment No. 7, particularly articles 1, 6 and 25.

Robert J. Smith (1991): 'Private Solutions to Conservation Problems,' in Tyler Cowen (ed.), *Public Goods and Market Failure: A Critical Examination*, New Jersey: Transaction Publishers.

3. Protecting the Environment with Property Rights, the Market and the Rule of Law
The Case Of Norilsk

Catherine Gillespie

Introduction

The importance of property rights, a market order and the rule of law in protecting the environment is well established in theory. When land is owned and ownership rights are protected through adequate rules, incentives are in place to ensure maintenance and protection. Decisions relating to property are subject to opportunity costs; and the true cost of destruction or wastefulness reverts to the owner, thereby discouraging such behaviour. It is when resources are free that there is no incentive to protect the environment. No personal cost is experienced if a river is polluted, for example, so there is no incentive to protect. Although the argument above has been made many times, and many other arguments exist to supplement the case for a free market approach to the environment, this approach is still not widely accepted.

To overcome this problem a more pragmatic approach is needed. I will argue for the importance of the free market in protecting the environment through a case study in Russia. Although it is instructive to examine cases of free market operation in Europe and the US, these examples are somewhat limited because they work within the framework of a government which legislates and directs behaviour towards the environment. A property rights approach may be saving some species of animal, or area of natural beauty, but opponents can argue that the very reason we have decided to value the animal, or the countryside, is because government legislation and direction has made us do so. Furthermore, within a framework in which extensive environmental legislation exists, it is difficult to prove the effects of property rights *ceteris paribus*. To prove the importance of property rights it is instructive to examine a case where there is little or no effective environmental legislation, and where the granting of property rights can be tracked and followed recently.

Such an example is Norilsk Nickel. This is a mining and metals complex located in Russia 200 miles north of the Arctic Circle. Norilsk Nickel is a holding company with six operating subsidiaries, which produce over 20 per cent of the world's total nickel output. It is also responsible for nearly 40 per cent of world platinum group metals (PGM) production. The real cost of this, however, is nearly sixty years of environmental destruction. By way of comparison, in 1995 Norilsk subsidiaries emitted 2.3 million tonnes of sulphur dioxide into the atmosphere, while Inco (the company's closest western competitor in terms of output) in the same year released only 436,000 tonnes. The result of such pollution is that hardly a tree is left standing for miles around the nickel complex. The environmental problems facing Norilsk are huge, but progress is beginning to be made. Furthermore, this progress can be linked directly to the privatisation of the company, and a basic extension of property rights, because there is no effective legislation in Russia at the moment which encourages environmental reform. Initially, it is necessary to give a brief history of Norilsk, and then to outline the effects that an extension of property rights and a primitive rule of law have had in beginning to transform the Norilsk complex and the surrounding area.

The History of Norilsk Nickel

The Norilsk complex is based in the Krasnoyarsk Krai region in East-Central Siberia. This is one of the richest natural resource regions in the world in terms of metals and oil and gas. However, Norilsk was not set up to make a profit from these huge resources. It was set up in the mid-1930s by Stalin as a regional centre for the administration of the Gulag network of concentration camps. The town of Norilsk has approximately 300,000 inhabitants and is perhaps the most extreme example of a factory town to be found in Eastern Europe. Activity in the town was entirely regulated by Moscow, including how much food was to be provided. Consequently, the town and Norilsk complex have been left without adequate transport or electricity, or the ability to produce enough food to sustain the population. The effect of this on the environment, as might be expected, has been devastating. Successive five-year plans measured the success of the company only in terms of output. This has had serious consequences. Firstly, metal was skimmed from the richest ore, leaving the remaining metal to be discarded as waste. This has littered the surrounding area with mountains of rich ore, and meant that shallow, unnecessary mines scar the countryside. Secondly, no price was put on wastefulness: people and resources have been squandered, and pollution has continued unchecked. This is a good example of the results of central planning on the economy and the environment. Norilsk belonged only to the state, and not even the workers had rights over their own actions or lives – when the ground thaws in spring the bodies of workers dumped in shallow ditches emerge. The only rule of law that existed was the arbitrary ruling of Moscow. The widescale destruction of the environment surrounding Norilsk is testament to the fact that no one had an interest in maintaining the countryside, so it went to waste. The question that must now be addressed is, how have property rights been introduced, and how has this affected the environment?

Recent Developments

Norilsk Nickel was transformed into a joint stock company in 1993, partly privatised in 1994, and fully privatised in 1997. One of the major shareholders is Unexim Bank, and the importance of private banks in the Russian restructuring process cannot be underestimated. Unexim Bank was founded in 1993 and has played an important part in returning state enterprises to profitability; among these are Sidanco, the oil concern, and Norilsk. One of the founding members of Unexim Bank, Vladimir Potanin, is now a member of the board of directors of Norilsk. This is important because it is evidence that the restructuring I will outline below is the work of private companies and individuals, who are motivated by the incentives provided by property rights and an emerging free market, and not by governments.

As part of the privatisation of the company, the surrounding town and other assets were also transferred to the company, in effect privatising every road, school and hospital in the process. The assets transferred to Norilsk included houses, roads, utilities such as electricity and gas, hospitals, schools, theatres and cinemas. The cost of maintaining these assets amounted to US$327 million in 1995. Although this might at first glance seem like a libertarian dream of mass privatisation, it is not. The cost of maintaining these social assets was too much for a company that was not, and still is not, breaking even. The fact that Norilsk was still liable for tax placed a further strain on maintaining the town. The simplest way to rid itself of the burden was for Norilsk to hand the town to the municipal government. The local government is also short of money, and cannot rely entirely on central government handouts. Lack of money is one of the main factors driving privatisation at a local and national level. The Federal Agency for Housing and Mortgage Lending was founded to encourage a mortgage market and house-buying throughout Russia. This means that inhabitants are beginning to buy their homes, and some effort is being made to sell off other sectors, mainly oil and gas. The privatisation is by no means complete, but the initiation of a property rights structure can be found. The new owners of Norilsk have an interest in seeing it become profitable, and the workers have a stake in the company through the shares they own. The inhabitants of Norilsk have a chance of owning their own houses, and have the power and incentives to change the area around them.

What Effects Has This Emergence of Property Rights Had?

The reforms that have been implemented at Norilsk have not been directly formulated with the environment in mind – this is not a problem, however. Improvement in environmental conditions has been a natural by-product of the pursuit of profit and efficiency, and the existence of property rights. This is of course completely contrary to the populist view that profit seeking and environmental protection are incompatible.

The restructuring plan had various basic aims, which have naturally improved environmental conditions: 1) To increase production from 177,000 tonnes of nickel in 1996 to 206,000 tonnes in 1997; 2) To employ managers who support reform; 3) To improve the international profile of the company in advance of an international equity issue planned for later this year; 4) To improve the efficiency of the company through investment in machinery and infrastructure.

The mines are being dug deeper to increase the yield per tonne of ore, and hence reduce the need to mine new open cast sites. New milling, smelting, and refining technologies have been developed which are slowly improving the efficiency of metal extraction and reducing environmental emissions. The amount of waste being sent for smelting is decreasing, which reduces the quantities of sulphur pumped into the atmosphere. Nickel concentrates are expected to increase by between 26-30 per cent, and copper concentrates are expected to increase from 20-25 per cent to over 30 per cent. In the refining process recovery rates from concentrates are expected to increase by 2-5 per cent. This will further economise on the consumption of materials in the process, and hence reduce emissions and other waste. One of the ironies is that Norilsk produces much of the world's PGMs, which the car industry in the west depends on for catalytic converters.

On a social level, environmental improvements are also being seen. Without orders from Moscow determining how much food and goods are to be produced, people have the incentives to start up cottage industries. Small shops are springing up to supplement the wages of the inhabitants, and are providing goods and services that people actually want. A few inhabitants have set up miniature brokering facilities to trade shares in Norilsk for local and international clients. The rates offered provide a 50 per cent discount to those on the Moscow Stock Exchange, which attracts a steady stream of business men from Moscow and abroad. The ownership of property, or at least greater control of property, is creating the incentives for people to clean up their town, and progress is being made. Of course, Norilsk will be a desolate, isolated and horrible place for a long time. The point is that the incentives are in place for environmental improvement and protection, and these incentives have been created through privatisation.

Norilsk illustrates a variety of points. The fact that without property rights disaster ensues does not require much proof, but the extent to which the government of the former Soviet Union has destroyed natural resources and the environment is often neglected. Partly this is understandable; some countries are still fighting internal wars, and facing such huge economic restructuring that the environment is often a secondary concern. Furthermore, the environmental problems are complex, as in the case of Norilsk, and caused by a variety of structural factors such as outdated technology which cannot be legislated away. Sites like Norilsk are also extremely inaccessible and unpleasant, providing little opportunity for a trendy Greenpeace PR shoot. The lack of legislation is not a bad thing as it allows us to use the case of Eastern Europe as a sign of what can happen if profit motives and property rights are introduced, and the effects this has on the environment. Once again it should be noted that it will be many years before Norilsk and other sites like it will be pleasant places, but a start is undeniably being made, and this start has been encouraged by privatisation.

The Rule of Law

The issue of the rule of law is a little more complex than that of property rights, as a rule of law is undeveloped in Russia. One of the main worries of fund managers investing in property is that there is no concrete guarantee that the government will not reclaim it. This is also a worry for investors in companies, although less so as the government simply cannot afford to buy back enterprises. The further Russia goes down the path of reform, the sooner such concerns will decline. Until a precise legal framework is in place to protect property and settle disputes, the incentives to improve the environment outlined above will remain limited. A system of property and tort law must evolve to provide a mechanism by which pollution can be prosecuted, and legal incentives must be put in place to encourage conservation. It can be argued that such a law is beginning to be developed on a local level, without strict control or legislation from Moscow.

Under the constitution adopted in 1993 a system of courts was set up, but with the exception of the constitutional court, the judiciary has little power. Although no defined legal structure has developed, the constitution allows the regions and territories a great deal of autonomy in legal and economic matters. A few territories may even raise their own army. This has resulted in a certain spontaneity and freedom in the way the regions conduct themselves. For example, local courts are settling disputes between companies as a matter of economic necessity. This could be the first sign of an adequate rule of law with respect to the environment. The workers and management of Norilsk have successfully settled pay disputes, and have reached agreement on working conditions. It does not seem too far-fetched to suppose that voluntary agreements taking the form of covenants, for example, might also be adopted to protect the environment. The incentives are there on both sides; for both workers and managers a more pleasant environment will bring benefits in health, general welfare, and the ability to attract foreign capital. Now that the owners of Norilsk – management, workers and investors – can determine the path the company can take, it is much easier to compromise on difficult issues, as the wage dispute resolution has shown. Local courts are beginning to take on a role in conflict resolution, so that in the future they can resolve environmental disputes and provide a mechanism to fine offenders. However, the inadequacy of the rule of law is testament to the importance of property rights and a growing market order; even without a rule of law that we would recognise, enough incentives are in place for restructuring to begin, and for people to feel the need to take care of the area they live in. Norilsk therefore seems to provide good evidence to prove that property rights and a market order are sufficient, on their own, to encourage protection of the environment.

Conclusion

The Norilsk mining company is not an isolated example – it is representative of the environmental results of central planning. However, with the introduction of law and property rights through capitalism the process of renewal has begun. Much of the former Soviet Union is riddled with cases such as Norilsk, and in other cases the incentives to improve environmental conditions are being provided by privatisation. Therefore it is clear that even after 70 years of collectivism and minimal exposure to market forces, the people in the region have been able to discover the tenets of market interaction: the rule of law, and private property. With these two institutions firmly in place, environmental conservation will have a foundation on which to flourish.

Questions and Objections

In this section I will try to deal briefly with some objections to my argument.

1) The example is a bit extreme – a factory in Siberia proves nothing about problems closer to home.

The example seems extreme only because we are ignorant of many problems outside Western Europe. Norilsk is a representative case – throughout the former Soviet Union environmental problems are beginning to be solved as capitalism takes root. This is directly relevant to discussions about the more developed world. Problems far worse than we can imagine are already beginning to be solved, while little progress is being made in other areas due to government interference.

2) The conditions were so bad originally that almost anything would have resulted in an improvement.

Although it is true that things could not have become much worse, had property rights not been established it is conceivable that there would have been no improvement. Furthermore, if legislation were awaited as the means to progress, there would have been no improvement either. The legislative process is necessarily slow, and results in one rule applying to all industry. No government policy would be able to capture the individual characteristics of each case. Therefore, it would prevent the best possible solutions arising through compromise, and would impose a solution which is inadequate for everyone.

3) The initial impetus has been provided by privatisation, but to really improve conditions we need government regulation.

Why should there be a need for regulation when, as I have shown above, most of the incentives are already in place to achieve results that are better for all the people affected. These incentives have resulted from a pursuit of profit and efficiency – the very thing environmental legislation seeks to curb. Legislation would also create opportunities for special interest groups, such as mining companies or environmental groups, to shape government policy in their own favour. This would destroy any incentive to reconcile conflicting interests, as is being done at the moment.

Bibliography

Grant Sinitskin (1997): *Norilsk Nickel – Cash Calf*, MC Securities/ United City Bank, 25 November.

Nikolai Arutyunov (1998): *A New Spring for Russian Reforms?*, Brunswick Warburg, 3 March.

Mark Pennington (1996): *Conservation and the Countryside*, London: Institute of Economic Affairs, Studies on the Environment No. 6.

Company research provided by Merrill Lynch, Nomura International and CentreInvest Securities.

For further discussion of property rights and the rule of law in the environment see:

Murray Rothbard (1977): *Power & Market*, Sheed, Andrews and McNeel.

Ludwig von Mises (1963): *Human Action*, New Haven: Regnery, Third Ed.

Ronald Coase (1974): 'The Lighthouse in Economics', *Journal of Law and Economics*, reprinted in Tyler Cowen (ed.), *Public Goods and Market Failures*, New York: Transaction.

Matt Ridley (1995): *Down to Earth*, London: Institute of Economic Affairs, Studies on the Environment No. 3.

– (1996): *Down to Earth II*, London: Institute of Economic Affairs, Studies on the Environment No. 7.

4. No More Toxic Beach Parties: The State of Britain's Beaches

Joseph Thomas

20 million people visit Britain's beaches each year. Each year, Britain's beaches are branded as horribly polluted by the press. 'Top beaches still too polluted for safe swimming', and 'Many beaches are cesspits' scream the headlines. Of course, these stories are denied by water companies and councils the country over, but who should the beachgoer believe, the fat cats and committees or the other most hated people of modern Britain?

The short answer is, believe what you read in the press. Not only do over one in ten bathing waters in the country fail to meet even the most basic pollution standards required by the European Union, but in several of our most popular holiday destinations this figure rises to 50 per cent. Add to this beaches littered with almost every conceivable kind of human debris, from lollipop sticks to condoms and hypodermic syringes, and the picture becomes clear: Britain's beaches are a hazard.

The implications of this sorry state of affairs are clear enough. Perhaps most seriously, people are getting ill. One group has had over 800 people register illnesses on its database, contracted directly as a result of swimming in polluted seawater.[1] Their problems are widespread, covering a range of infections and problems. The breakdown is displayed in Figure 1.

If people get ill by going swimming in the sea, they are clearly less likely to want to visit the seaside. This brings problems for local economies built around tourism. It is no mistake that while more people *are* taking holidays in Britain, they are opting for the 'detox' atmosphere of Centre Parcs rather than the likes of Blackpool and Brighton. The results of this natural tendency are that traditional employment in coastal areas has fallen, and that

---

[1] Surfers Against Sewage Medical Database.

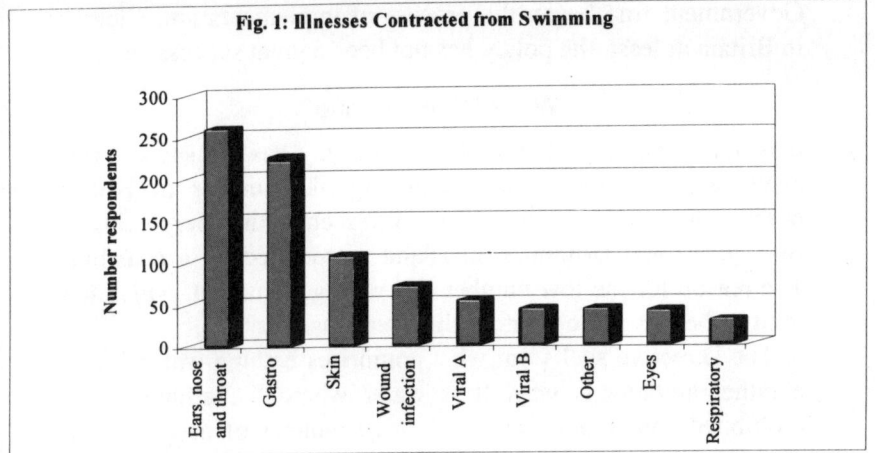

Source: Surfers against Sewage Medical Database.

beachfront B&Bs are being gradually commandeered by the DSS.

The Present Framework

A number of people, undoubtedly with good intentions, have tried to rectify the situation. They have done so by enacting laws, the principal one of which is an EU directive, 'Council Directive 76/160/EEC concerning the quality of bathing water.'

Cutting through the legal jargon, the crux of the law is that per sample of water taken, bathing water, either coastal or inland, must contain no more than given levels of coliforms, bacteria generally accepted as being indicators of sewage. In addition to this, the Directive outlines more rigorous guideline levels of coliforms, laid down as a benchmark to which member states should aspire. The Directive was issued in 1975 and laid down a time limit of 10 years, after which member states were to be fully compliant. In other words, in 1985, British beaches should have had an almost 100 per cent 'hit rate' in passing the test.

Figure 2 shows that in 1985 Britain was a long way from achieving even this basic objective. Then, the 'hit rate' for British beaches was over 20 per cent lower than it should have been, having barely improved since 1979, when the British

Government first began the process of implementation. Clearly, in Britain at least, the policy has not been a great success story.

What Went Wrong?

It is noticeable from Figure 2 that not only has the success rate been very low, but in the beginning, the number of British beaches was very low too. This may seem rather perplexing at first, given that Britain is an island surrounded by a coastline. The reason for the low number lies with government, which has tried its best over the years to shirk responsibility.

The Directive spells out what comprises bathing water, but in a rather ambiguous way. It is water where '...bathing is not prohibited and is practised by a large number of people.' This imprecise description has left the UK Government in a position where it has been able to adopt its own very restrictive definitions of what it believes UK bathing waters are. This is the reason why, in the early 1980s, the farcical position emerged of there being only twenty-seven official UK bathing waters, *fewer than in Luxembourg*, which is the smallest country in the EU and landlocked to boot. The UK definition was so restrictive that the list of official bathing waters excluded both Blackpool and Southport. Things eventually did change when European pressure was put on Britain and the UK Government was taken to court.

The reason for this lack of government enthusiasm for improving beach quality could be put down to several factors. Some might argue that government has higher priorities and that the environment is at best a marginal issue. The more cynical might add that government reticence stems from other reasons. While government itself is not directly affected by pollution, just being slapped on the wrists every so often for getting it wrong, actually dealing with the problem and failing beaches serves to attract negative attention, having much more direct implications on electoral prospects. Given this choice, the politician's best strategy is clearly to do nothing.

Local government is also to blame. In seaside areas, two of the most important functions of the local authorities are coastal management and promotion of the area to tourists. Unfortunately, the authorities can easily find themselves in a position where

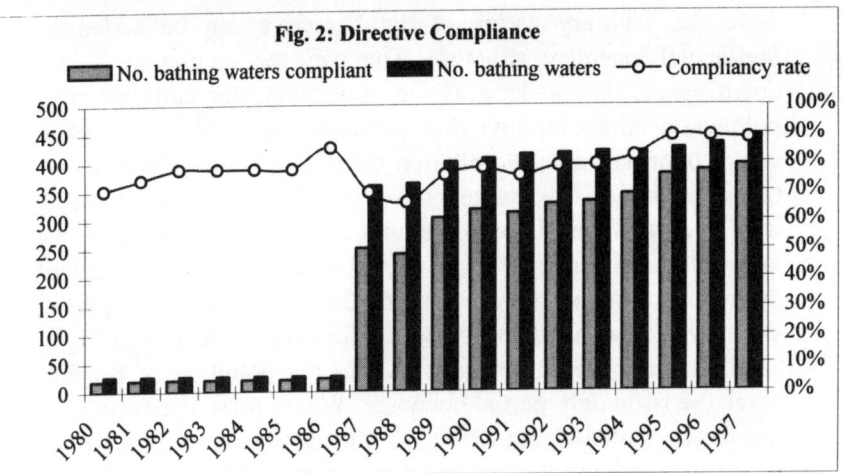

Source: Environment Agency

these two functions are pulling in opposite directions. That is to say, achieving high quality beaches is not necessarily helpful in attracting tourists. If local authorities have to pursue court actions against polluting water companies, they must first admit that there is a problem, putting potential tourists off taking their holiday there. In this situation, local authorities have found it in their best interests just to ignore the problem and hope that no one notices. Where inertia is the order of the day, problems can easily to go from bad to worse, as the polluters have no incentive to stop polluting.

But the failure of Britain to produce reasonably clean beaches and bathing waters is due to more than just failure of British Government. The Directive itself is problematic. Of the illnesses recorded on the database above, 72 per cent were from beaches *passing* the mandatory EU standards, indicating that the maximum statutory levels are, at best, arbitrary. This arbitrariness is unsurprising given that the regulation was the result of a political bargaining process, subject to interference from all manner of interest groups. The resulting outcome is not necessarily the best for public health, for business or anything else, but it is the most politically attractive compromise between the sides.

To the arbitrary nature of the Directive can be added an ineffectual incentive structure. The way the regulation is laid down means that so long as the mandatory standards are met, polluters need not improve their performance. Clearly, in a world where improvements in pollution control technology are always being made, this is somewhat perverse. One way, however imperfect, that the EU could attempt to remove this defect in the law would be to update it on a regular basis to take account of these improvements. However, 76/160/EEC has not been updated since 1975. The law does not say anything about beach litter.

In all then, the current approach to the pollution of beaches gives the issue only partial coverage. Where there is coverage, it has largely failed owing to the arbitrary nature of the regulations being imposed and the failure of government to enforce the law on what is largely seen as a peripheral issue in British politics.

The Property Rights Solution

In the absence of effective government stewardship, European regulation has been the tool used to improve the quality of Britain's beaches, the constraint stopping standards falling below a certain level. This has been shown to be of little practical use in improving British standards. A better constraint would be one imposed by beach users themselves. They know what they are willing to tolerate much better than a bureaucrat located several hundred miles away, applying 'one size fits all' regulations to fifteen member states, landlocked or otherwise.

But how should users translate opinion into action? One possible way would be by having environmental regulations made on a more regional basis, invoking the principle of subsidiarity. However, although this may improve the situation at the margin, the problem will remain that beach users are just one more party at the political dealing table, competing against the water companies, environmentalists and the rest. Being more dispersed and less well organised than these other groups, beach users would tend to find themselves at a disadvantage and coming away with less-than-ideal results, even though the regulations are apparently being made for their benefit.

The best way of overcoming such problems, inherent in any negotiating process, is by taking the issue of beach and bathing water pollution out of the sphere of politics altogether and putting it in the realm of private action. Only the large scale privatisation of Britain's coastline, putting land ownership in the hands of private parties, will provide beach users with the clarity of voice that they have for so long lacked.

Perhaps the most obvious tool for this improvement in a private system is the marketplace. Beaches provide a service to their users, which although intangible is very real. This service could be charged for by beach owners, making beaches potentially profitable. To realise any such profit, owners must first be able to attract large numbers of customers on to their stretch. Customers do not like littered and polluted beaches, so it would be in the very best commercial interests of the owners to ensure that this was not the case.

Litter would be the easiest issue to resolve for private owners, as they have direct control over how frequently it is collected and the provision of litter bins. Pollution in bathing waters would be more difficult as it is generally produced not as a result of the owner's activity, but by the activity of others, particularly water companies. The problem would not be insurmountable, though the owners obvious resort when subject to any such pollution would be tort law, prosecuting polluters for their nuisance and stopping the pollution.

So, by using beaches as the commercial resource that they potentially are, the necessary incentives would be in place to ensure that beaches are kept clean. Failure to do so could result in serious financial losses for the owners, focusing their minds much more effectively than government ever focused its own. Because it is ultimately beachgoers themselves who police a system based on private property, they would be in a position to demand improvements in water and beach quality, to be listened to and accommodated.

But the marketplace is not the only mechanism by which a private system could maintain effective stewardship of Britain's beaches. An obvious alternative is that, in certain areas, the voluntary sector could take over beach management. This would be particularly likely in areas of particular natural interest, where many charities have considerable expertise. A private system could accommodate charities wishing to buy and conserve the coast just as easily as it could accommodate those wishing to use it for profit.

The two possibilities for coastal management – one commercial, one charitable – are not mutually exclusive. In fact, in a system of private beach ownership, both would probably run simultaneously, with different organisations concentrating on the areas that they manage the best.

A number of criticisms may be raised to this scheme. Perhaps the most forthcoming would be that it is based on a great deal of conjecture. Are people *really* willing to pay for a day at the beach, something that has always been free in the past? Would the law *really* be effective in stopping pollution? Would the voluntary sector *really* buy and manage beaches?

The last point is perhaps the easiest to answer yes to. It is being done and has been done for years. Groups such as the RSPB have an admirable track record of buying land and preserving it, even buying damaged land to restore it (Ridley, 1996). There is no reason why what has been done inland should not also apply to the coast.

On the issue of people being willing to pay to use beaches, the answer is again in the affirmative. A 1990 study in the US found that the value of a day at the beach is $33.91 per person. Clearly, there are major cultural differences between the UK and US, so this figure would not be directly applicable here, but if people are willing to pay for petrol to get to the seaside, and to pay for parking and ice creams, they would presumably pay to go on a beach when they got there.

The question of whether the law could accommodate a system whereby beach owners could sue polluters has recently also been answered with a decisive 'yes.' In 1993, one of the few private beach owners in the UK took South West Water to court after a period in which faecal material, condoms, panty-liners and sanitary towels covered his 1.2 km stretch of lawns and beaches. The waste led to one surfer collapsing in a coma and possibly the death of another from viral pneumonia. The beach owner brought the civil proceeding in respect of nuisance and trespass and claimed £1 million for clean-up costs and lost revenue (*The Independent*, 1994).

The case was a landmark one, and was the first time that a private individual managed to force a water company to make improvements on their sewage system. Additionally, although the final settlement was out of court, the speed with which the beach owner managed to get the issue resolved was thought remarkable by the law journals (*Water Law*, 1994). This sets an impressive benchmark against which any system of privately-owned beaches could operate in the future. In fact, under a fully private and competitive system of beach ownership, action would probably be taken earlier by beach owners who fear bad press causing long-term damage to their reputations.

Another set of objections raised to the plan include fears about how such a system could provide beachgoers with sufficient information to make the appropriate decisions in the absence of government intervention, and how less popular coastal areas could maintain high quality beaches in the absence of fierce competition.

The second of these arguments is, to a degree, spurious. It may be true that, under a private system, pollution standards vary around the country and that the less popular areas of the coast end up with higher levels of pollutants in their bathing waters. However, this is actually the efficient response of the market to the desire to maintain human safety as it means that abatement policies are being targeted where they are needed the most – where people are actually swimming.

The first argument is more interesting. It is true that beachgoers cannot behave rationally without sufficient information to make their decisions, and a scenario where insufficient information is provided could theoretically exist. In practice, however, the situation would not arise – there is a market for the provision of information about beaches.

The beach information market is being serviced already, and beachgoers can obtain their information from a variety of sources. *The Reader's Digest* publishes a 'Good Beach Guide' each year. Another organisation doing something similar is the Tidy Britain Group. Operating in conjunction with the European Union's 'Blue Flag' scheme and with the Seaside Awards, the group assesses the quality of all beaches, both 'resort' and 'rural', on the criteria of safety, quality of management, cleanliness, water quality and information provision. Such groups would most probably take on a much more important role in a private system. Refusal of beach owners to allow them to inspect would not be looked on favourably by the paying public. There is therefore no reason to doubt that information would be efficiently provided.

Whither Now?

The UK is now in an ideal position to move towards a private property system of coastal management. Not only is the infrastructure in place to make the transition a smooth one – the information providers are up and running and the laws on pollution are favourable to private beach managers – but the trend against domestic holidays has faded for the first time in many years. This gives potential beach entrepreneurs genuinely rosy business prospects.

Unfortunately, there is still a small matter of EU law to deal with. It overrides national laws and therefore cannot be removed easily. However, it should not prove a barrier to the implementation of a system which would probably raise standards well above the EU ones anyway. It just means that government will have to continue to be involved over the transition, while all parties concerned are given time to adjust fully. While this may be a hindrance, it is not fatal.

Beaches and the sea will never be perfectly clean. In terms of pollution, two seagulls are equivalent to one human being and no one is suggesting that either should be banned from the seaside. At least under a system of coastal management based on private property rights, the incentives would be in place to remove the worst excesses.

References

The Independent (1994): 16 April.

Matt Ridley (1996): 'The Need for Conservation Entrepreneurs', in *Down to Earth II*, London: Institute of Economic Affairs, Studies on the Environment No. 7.

Water Law (1994): November.

Bibliography

Jerry Taylor (1997): *Environmentalism and Liberty: Where the Twain Might Meet*.

Journal of Environmental Law, Vol. 6, No. 1.

The Daily Telegraph, 22 April 1996, 22 May 1997.

The Times, 17 June 1994.